I0846310

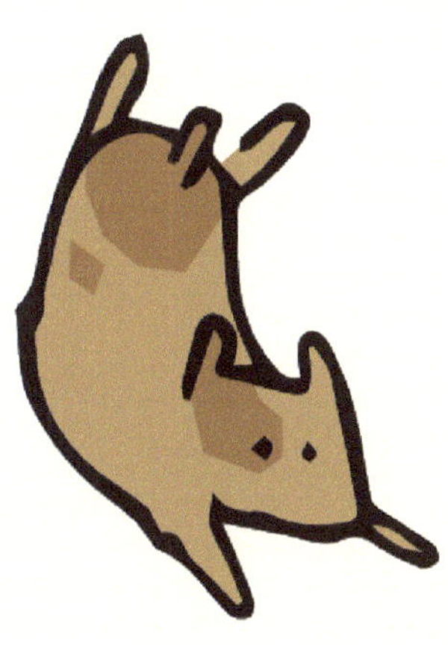

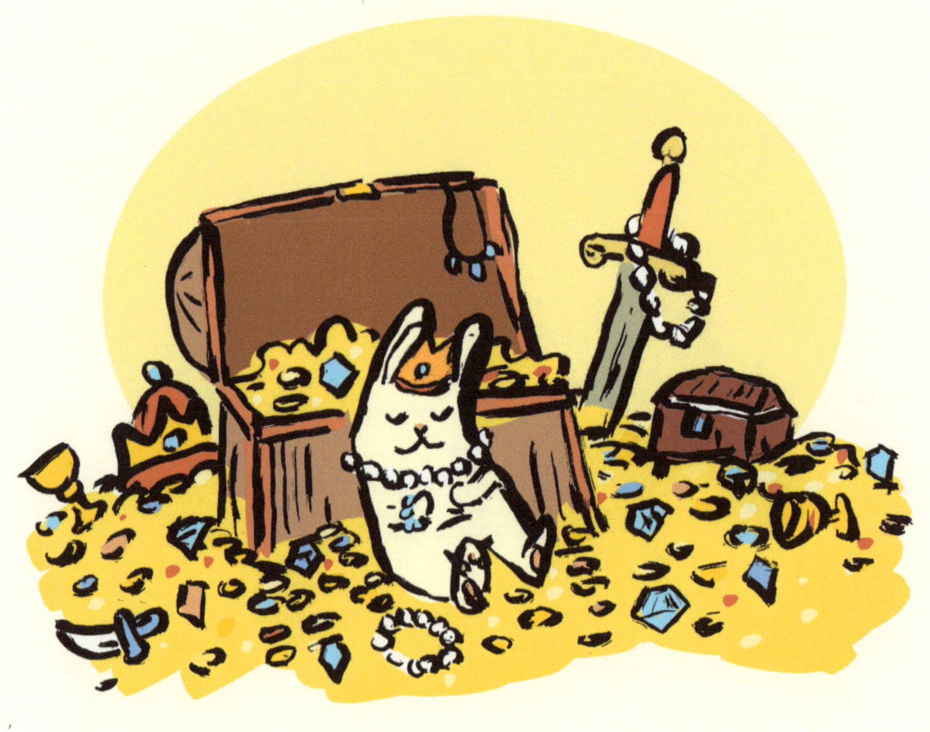

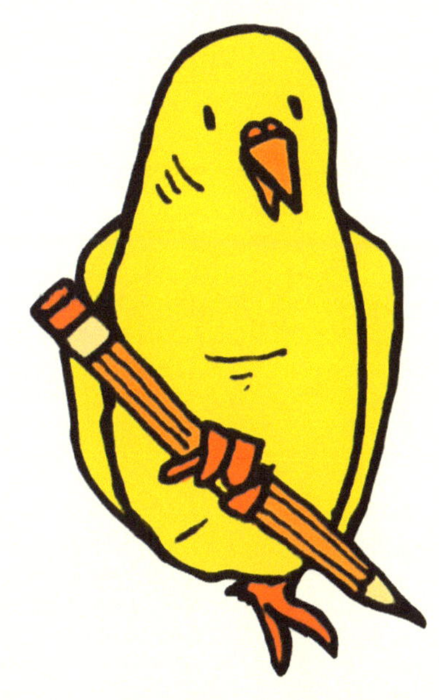

Tina Timm
Illustrator   Cartoonist
Portfolio

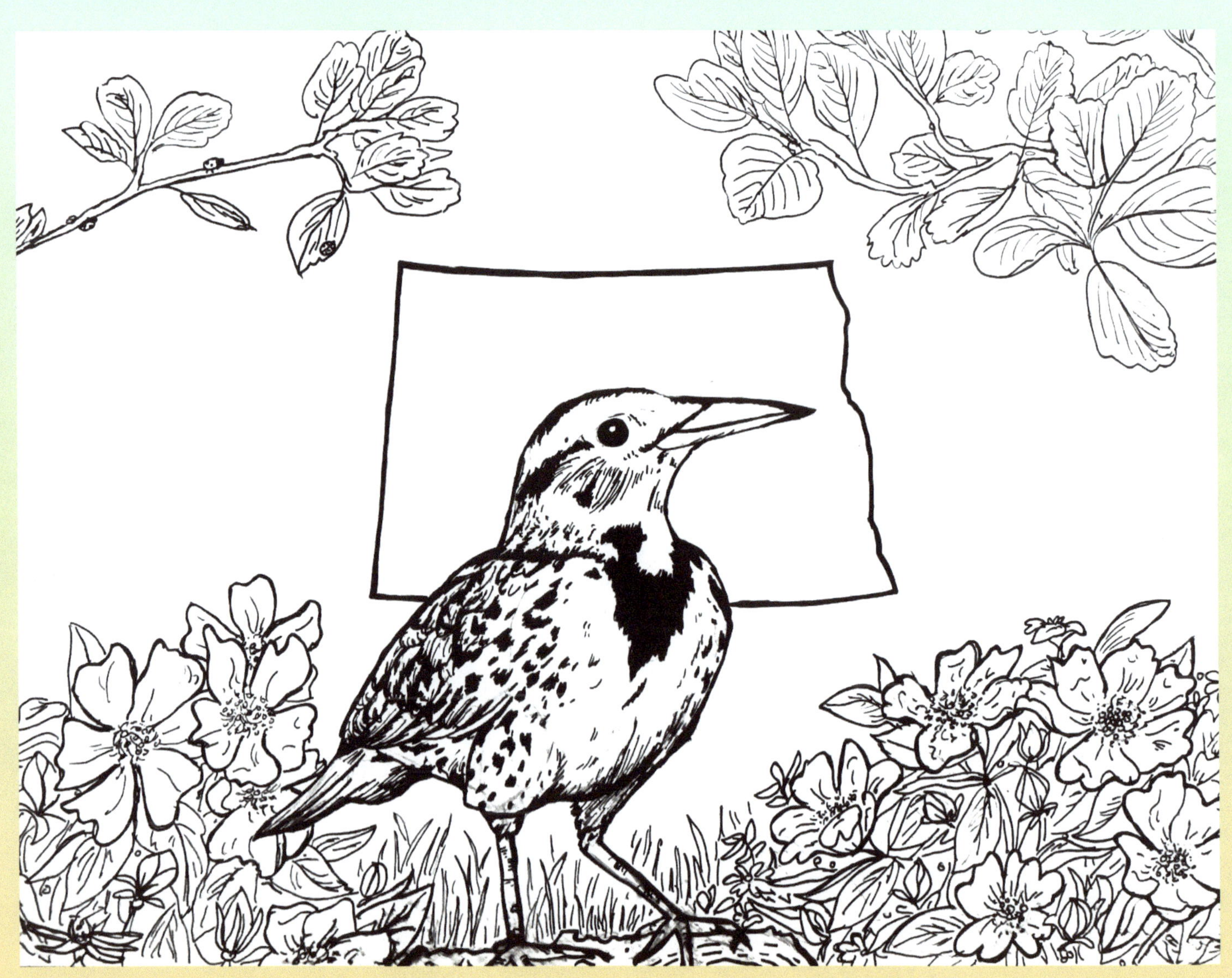

The Symbol of North Dakota, 16 x 20 in, 2023

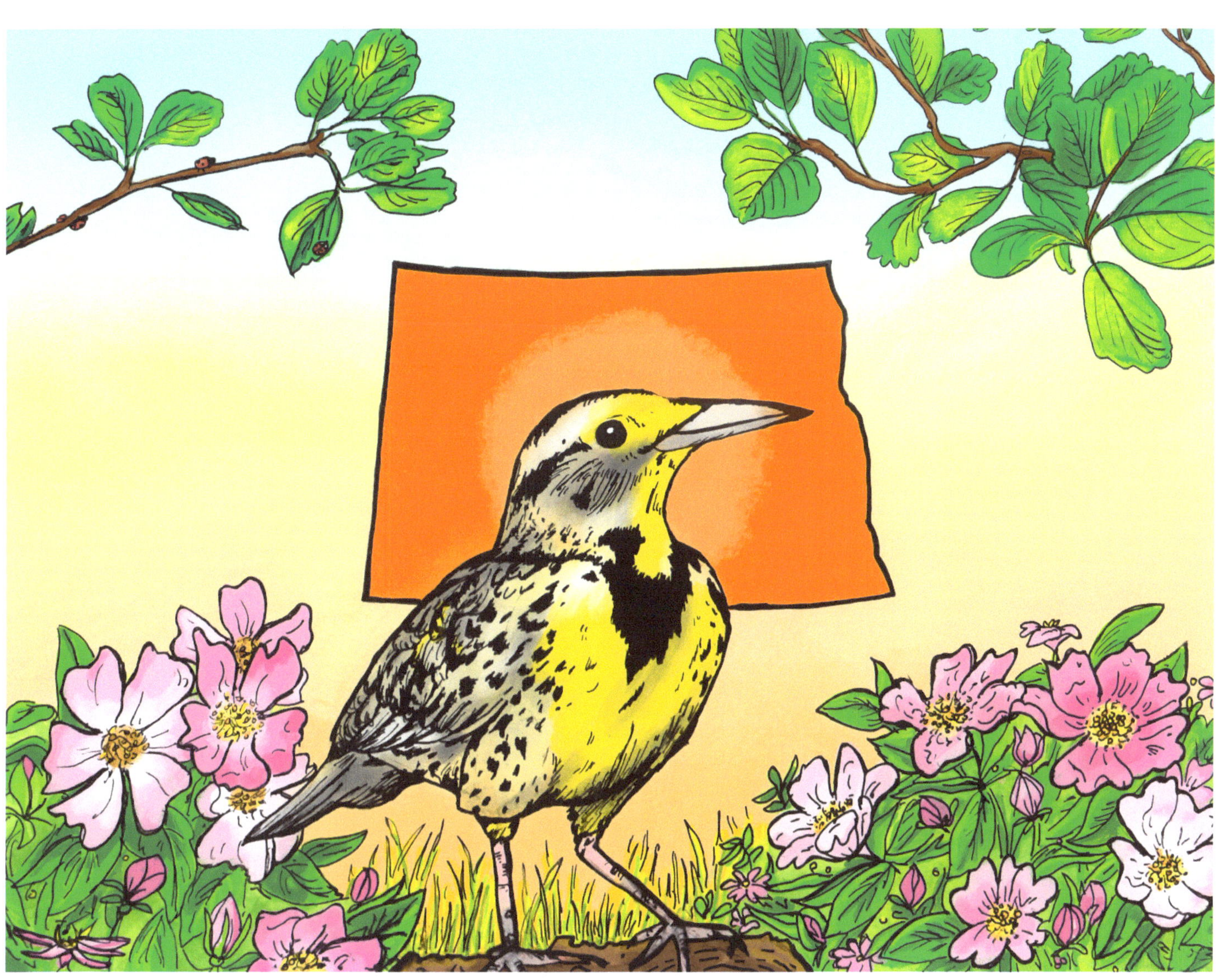

The Symbol of North Dakota, 16 x 20 in, 2023

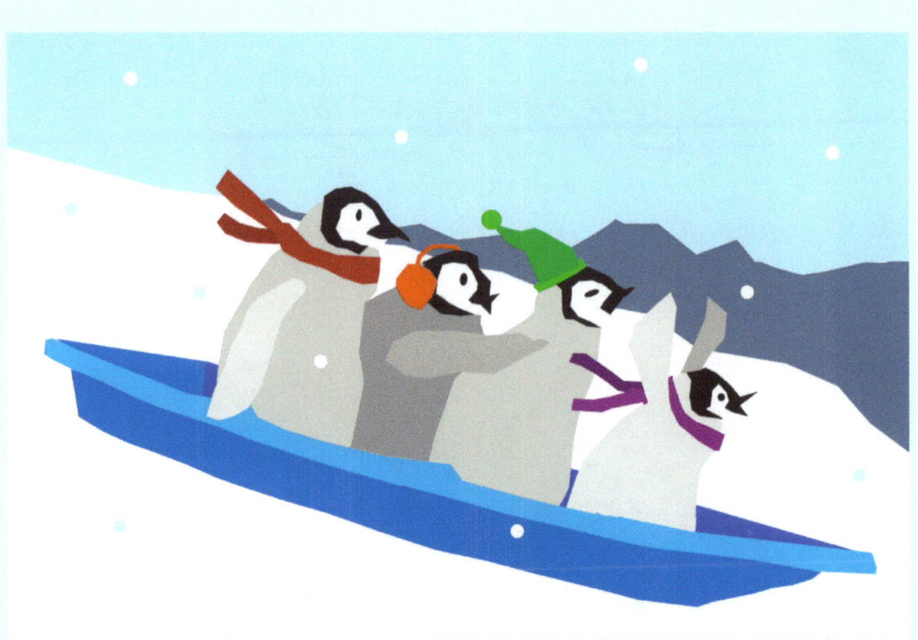

A Snowy Day, 4 x 6 in, 2021

Wonders of Antarctica

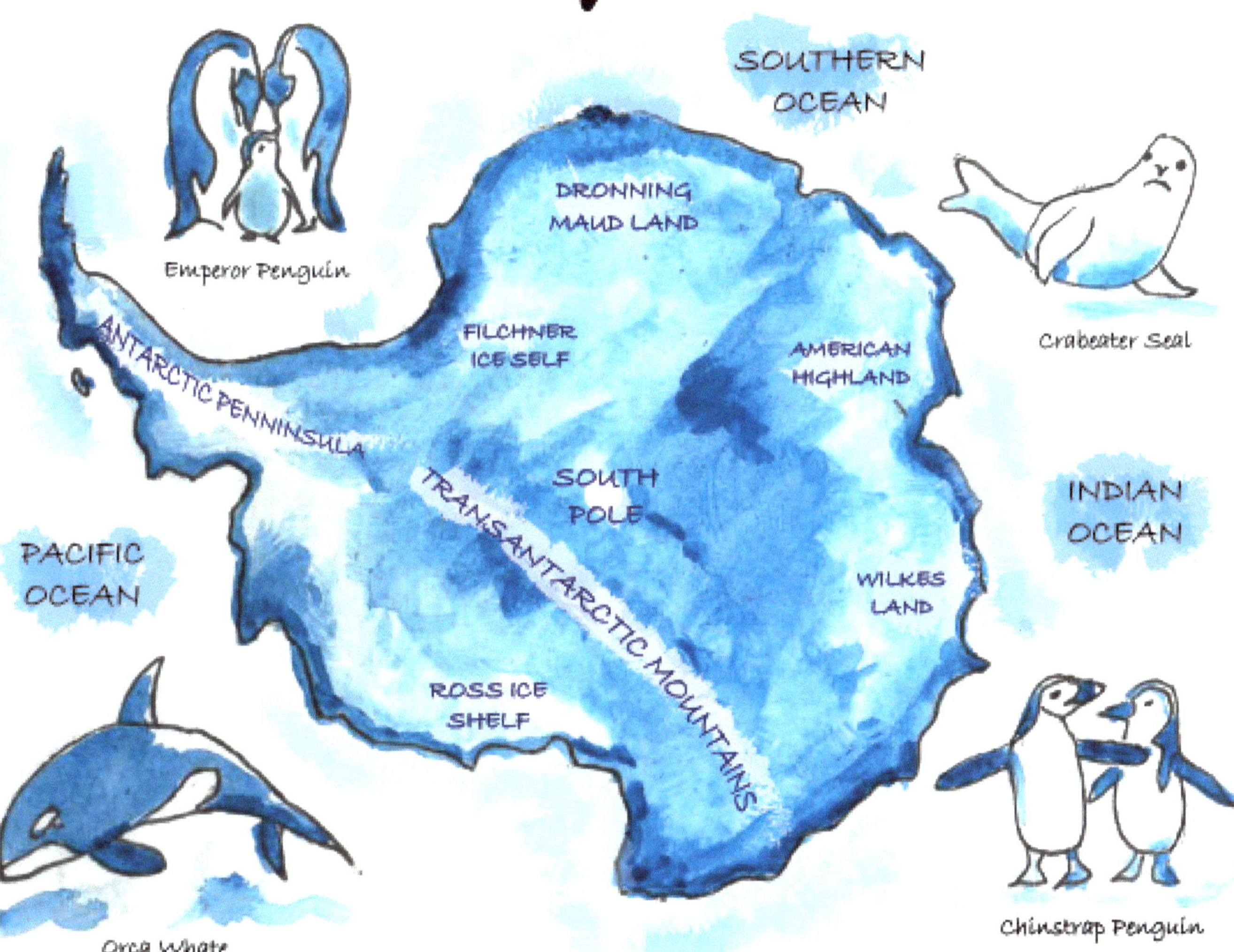

Antarctica is a continent full of beauty and mystery. The continent wasn't seen by human eyes until 1820! You have to be tough to live in this environment because Antarctica is the driest, coldest, and windiest place on Earth. Despite this, Antarctica is home to many species of penguins, seals, and gulls. Whales and narwhals are also common creatures swimming by the coast. Today, no country has claims to the continent because it is a neutral ground for study and research.

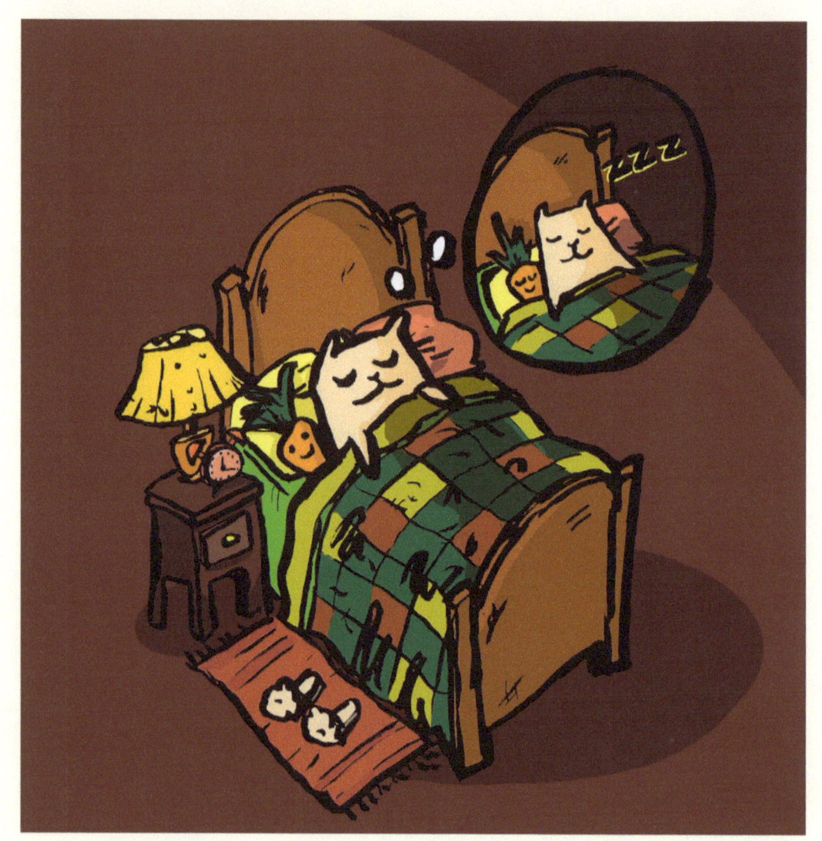

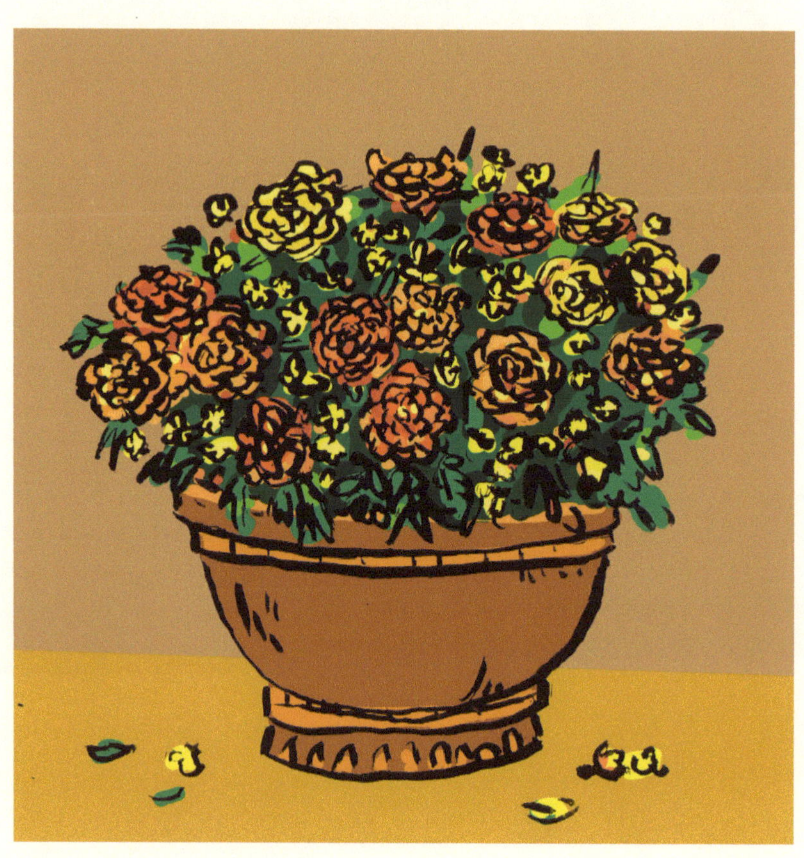

Inktober - Dream (above) Golden (below), 8 x 8 in 2023

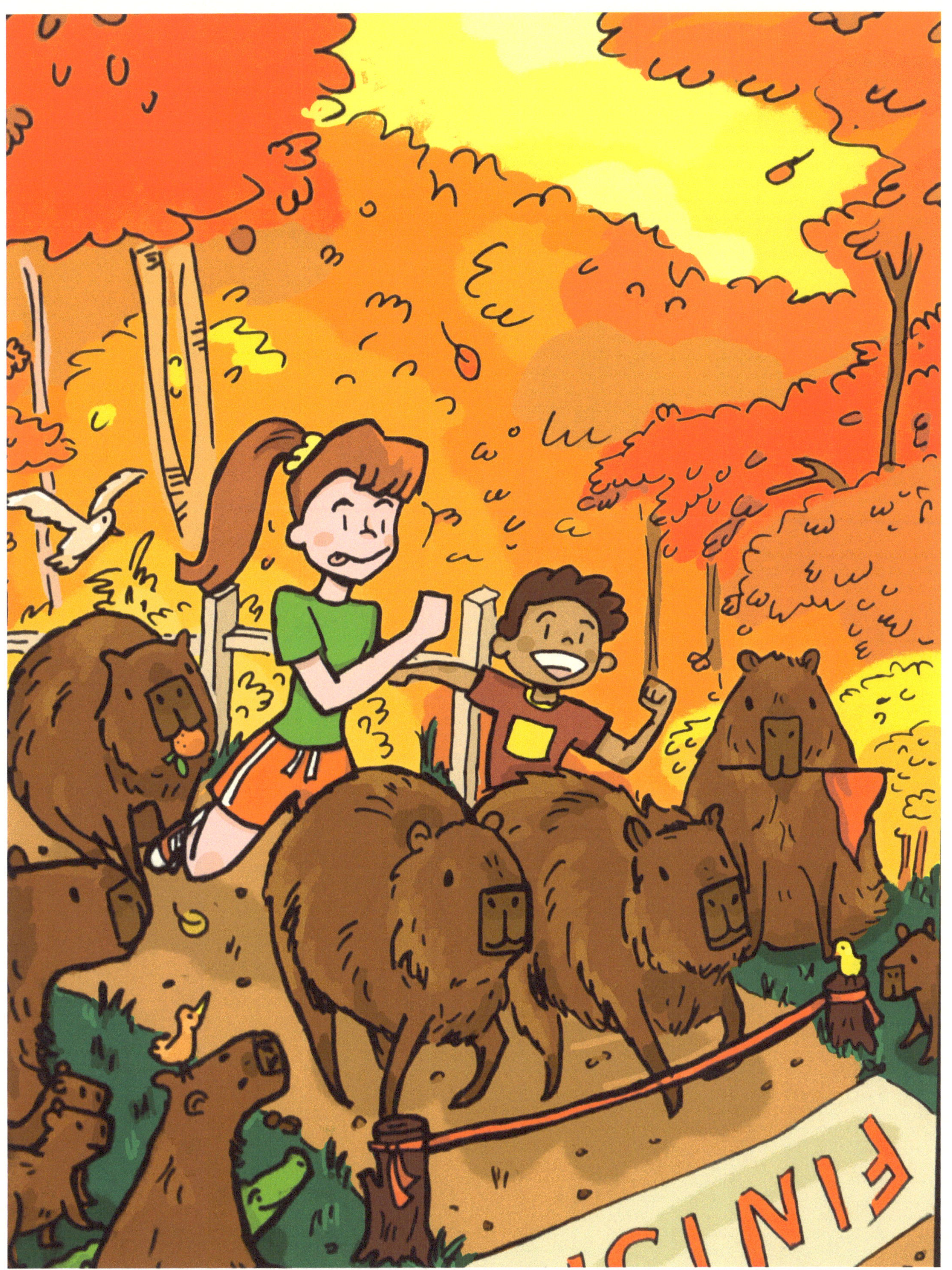

Capybara Race 8 x 11 in, 2023

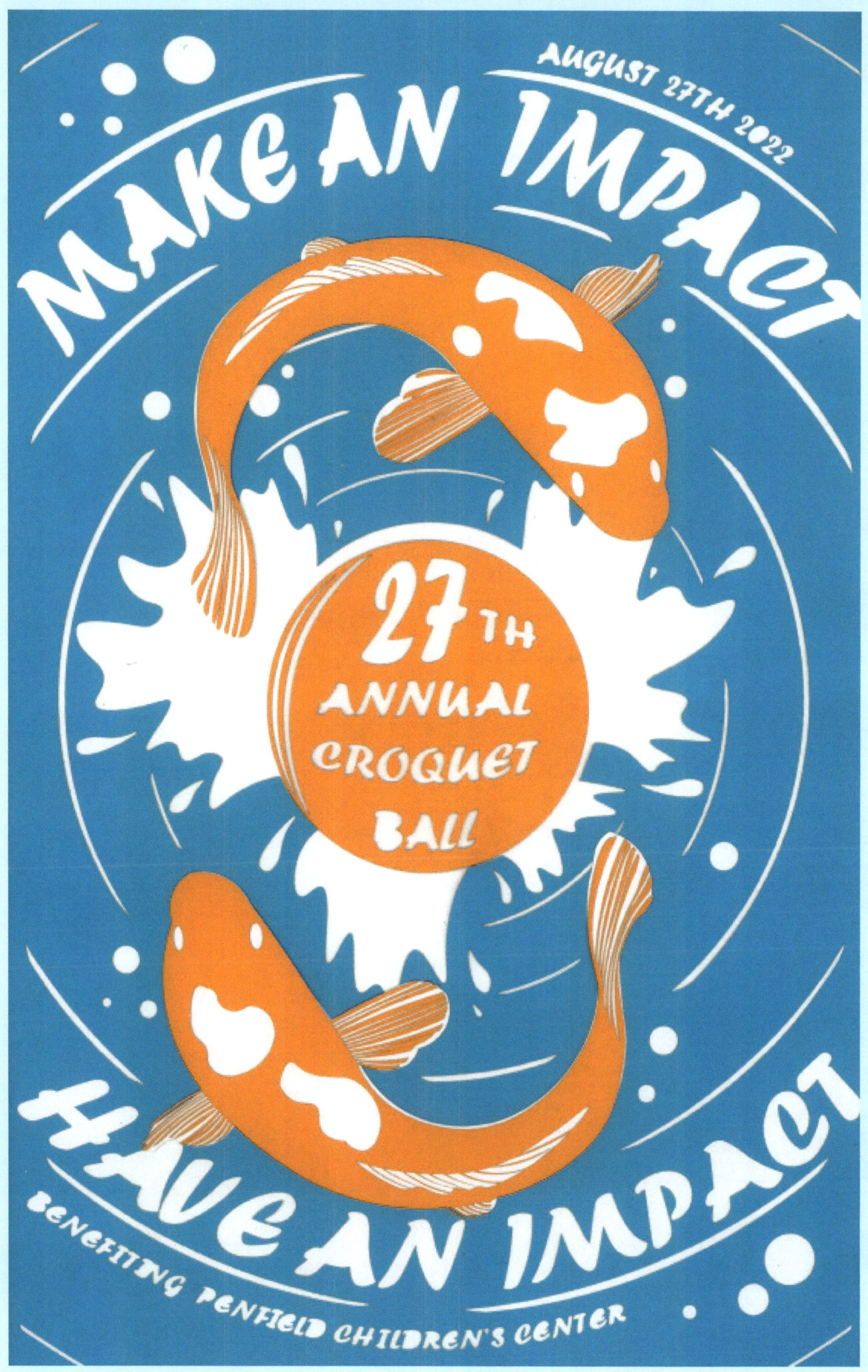

Penfield Children's Center, Make an Impact, 24 x 36 in, 2022

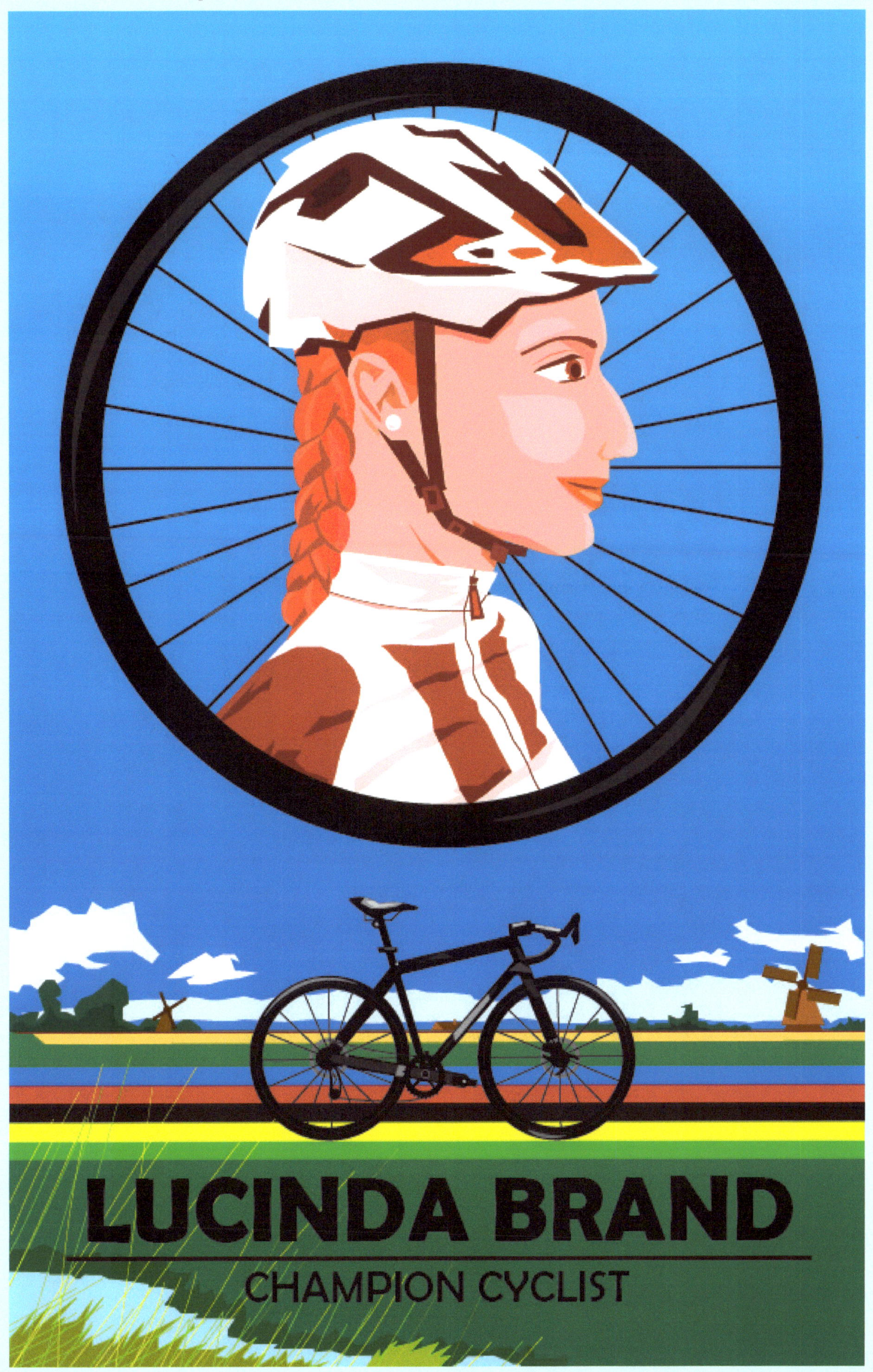

Lucina Brand ,Trek Bikes, 24 x 36 in, 2022

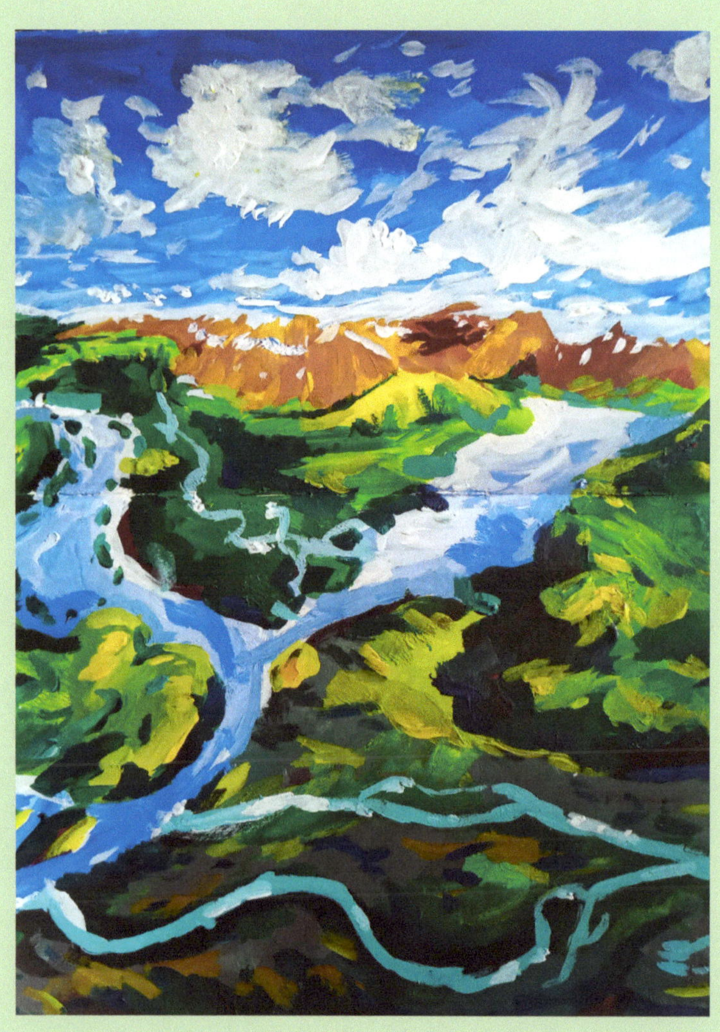

Iceland Sunrise, 5 x 8 in, 2021

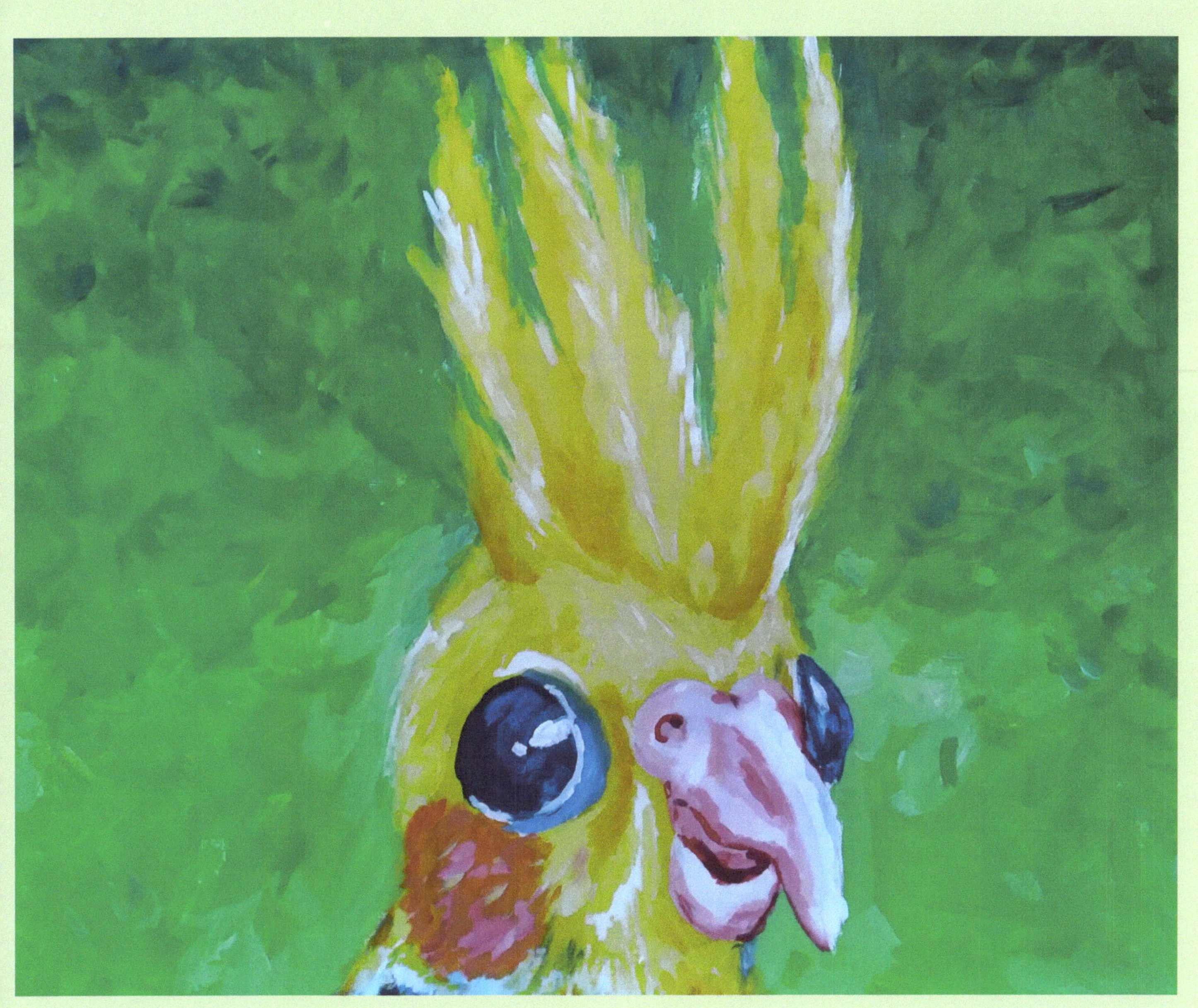

Cockatiel Suprise, 18 x 24 in, 2021

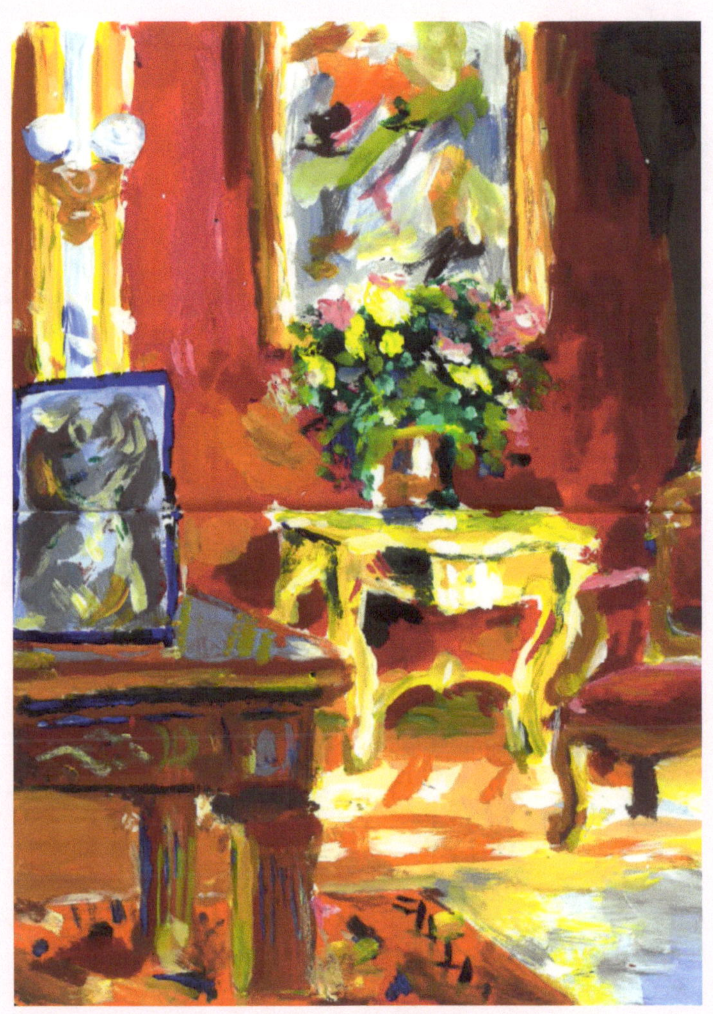

Iceland Sunrise, 5 x 8 in, 2021

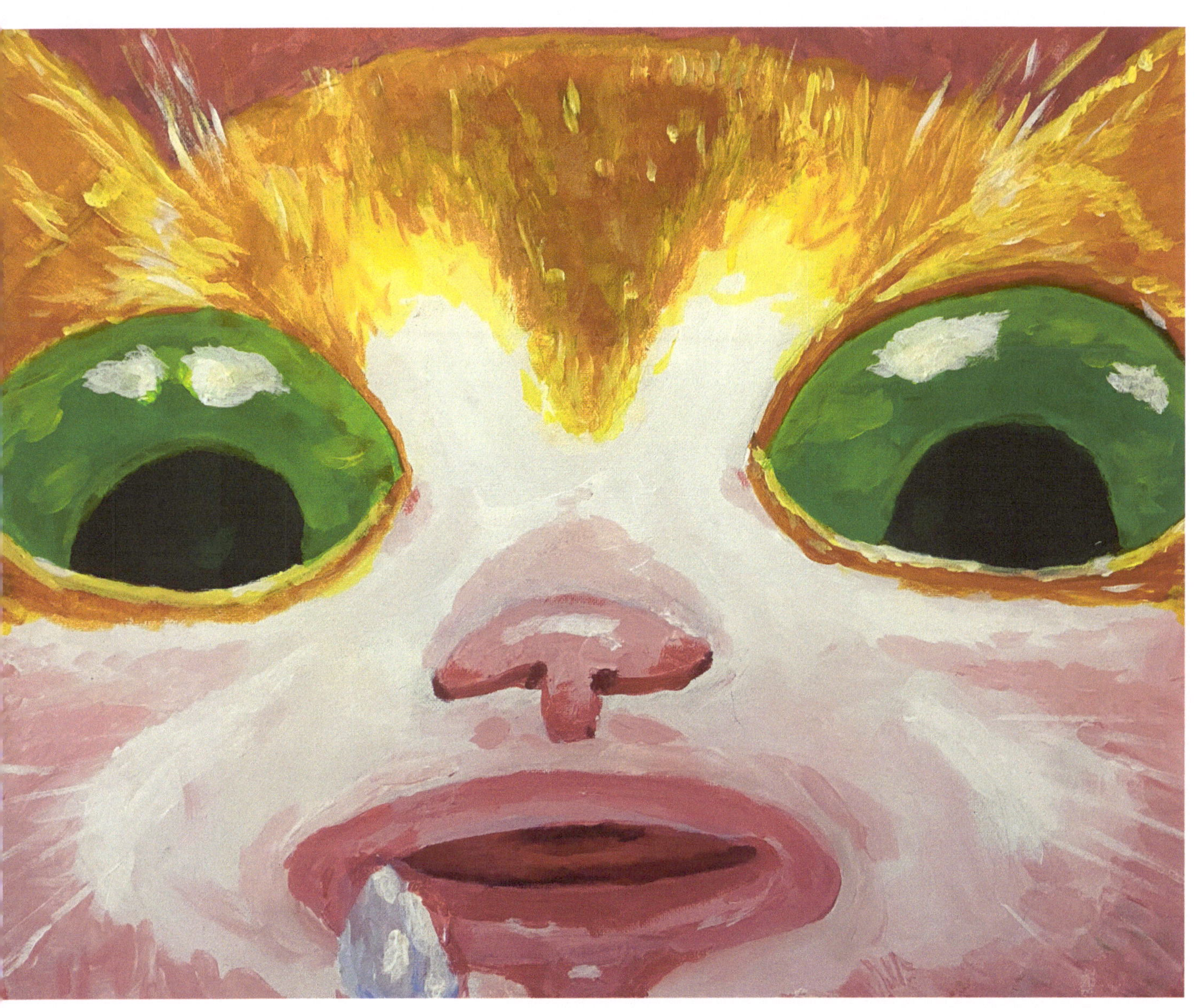

Googas, 18 x 24 in, 2021

Honey Bee, 10 x 10 in, 2023

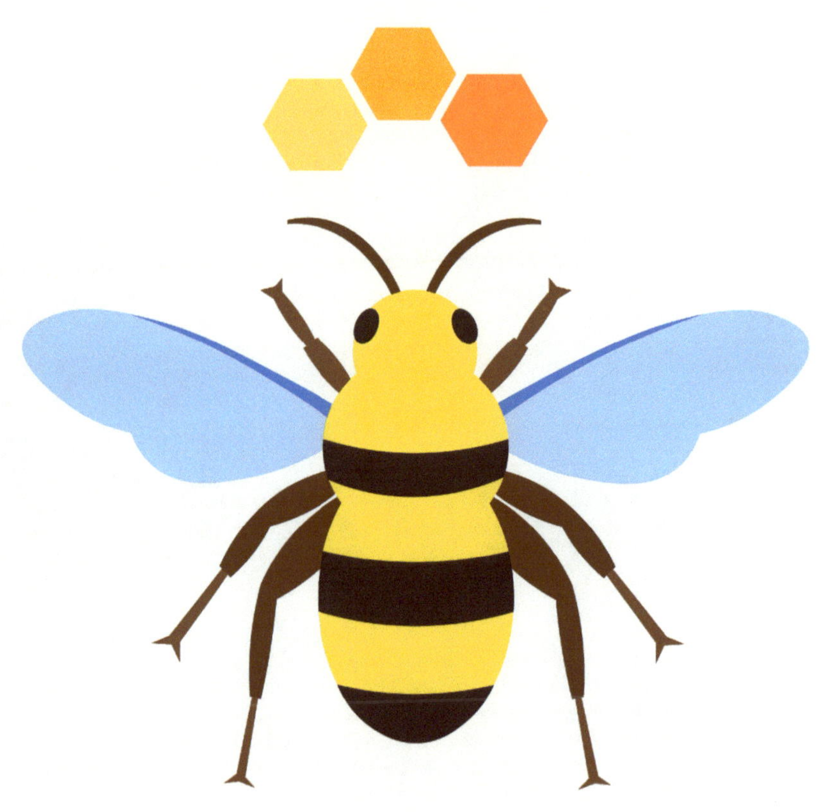

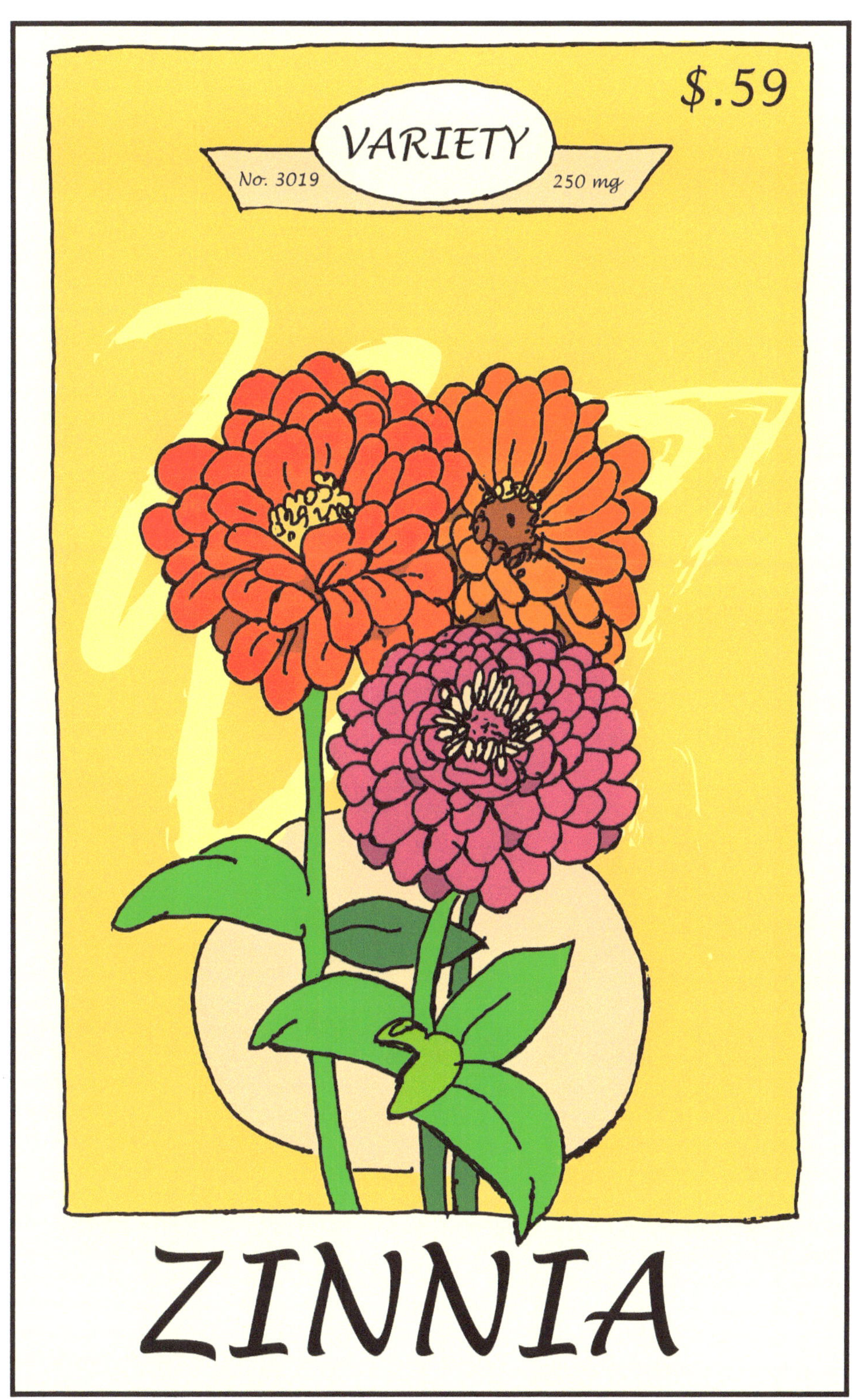

Zinna Flower Packet, 7 x 11 in, 2023

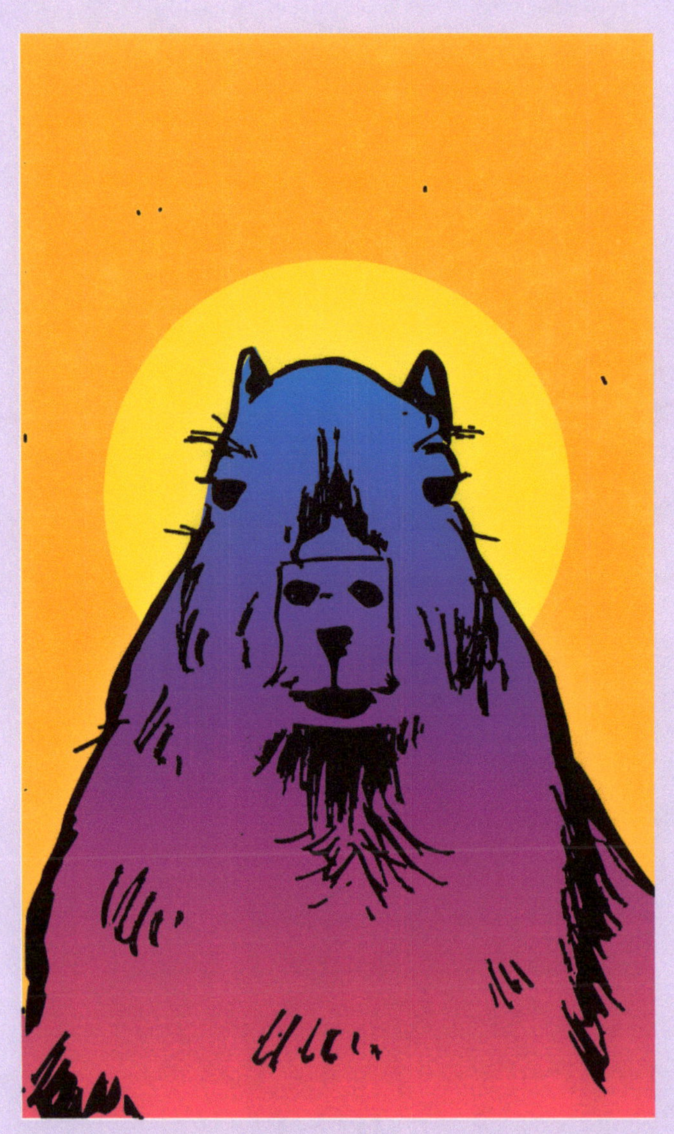

Amazing Capybara, 5 x 8 in, 2022

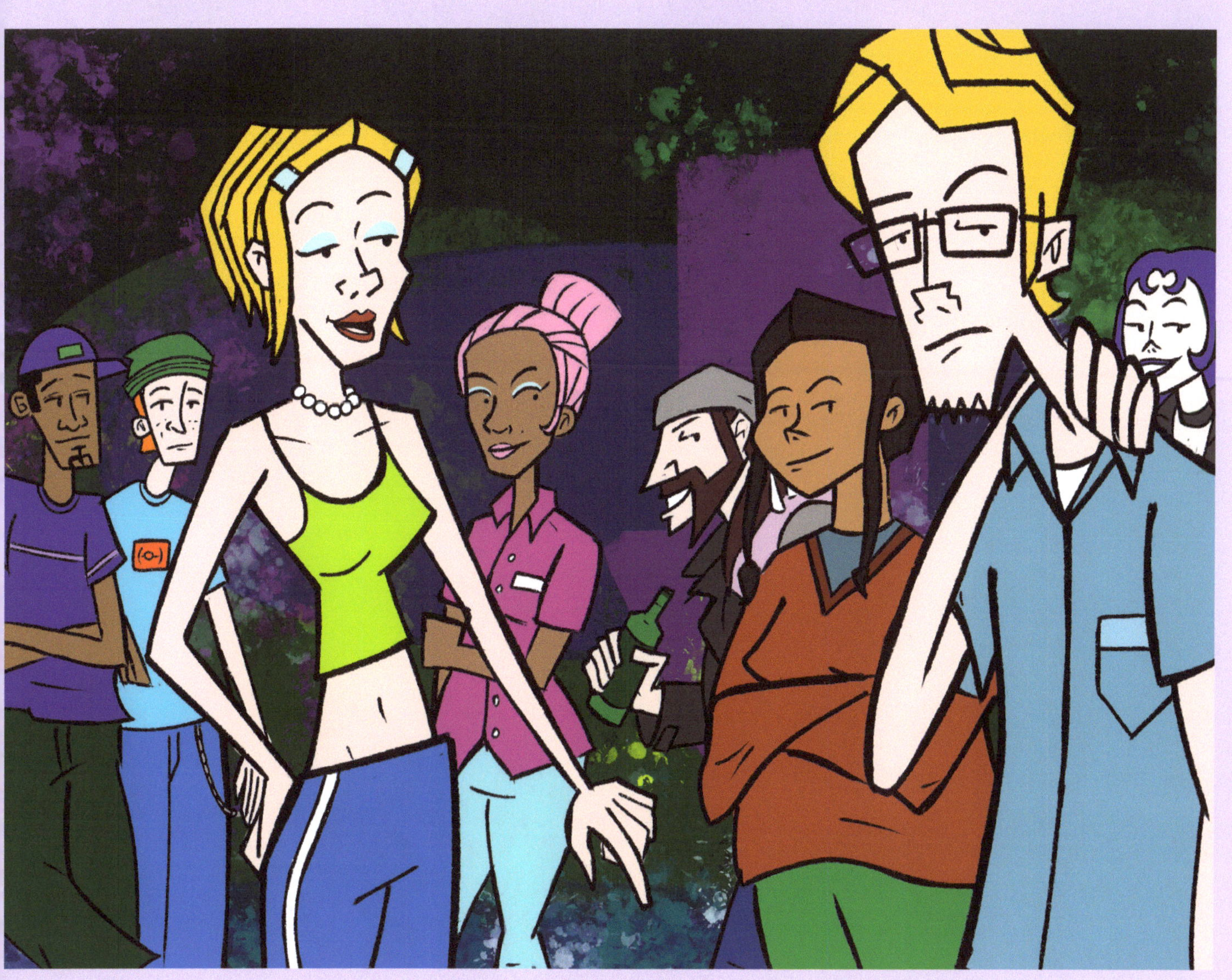

Downtown, 12 x 8 in, 2023

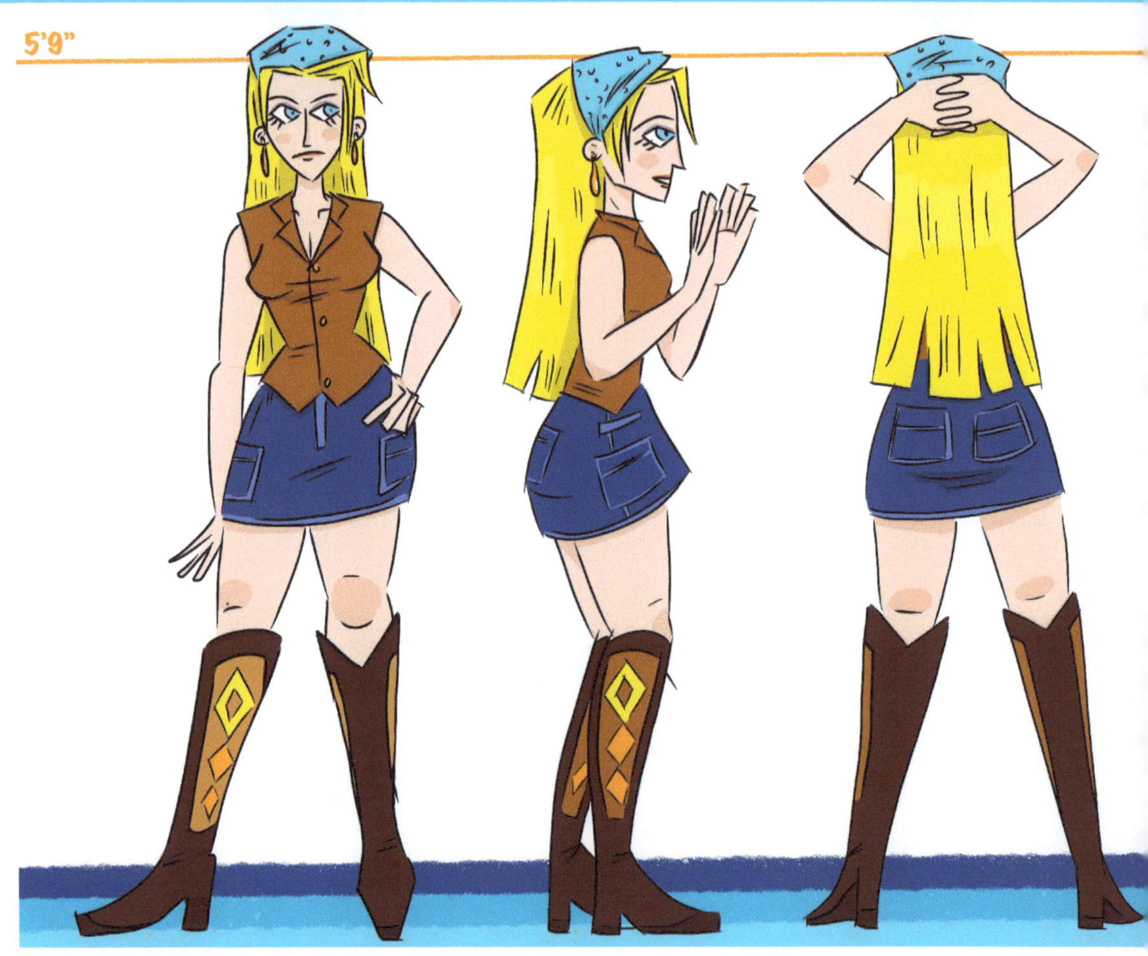

Martha Character Sheet, 4096 x 1714 px, 2023

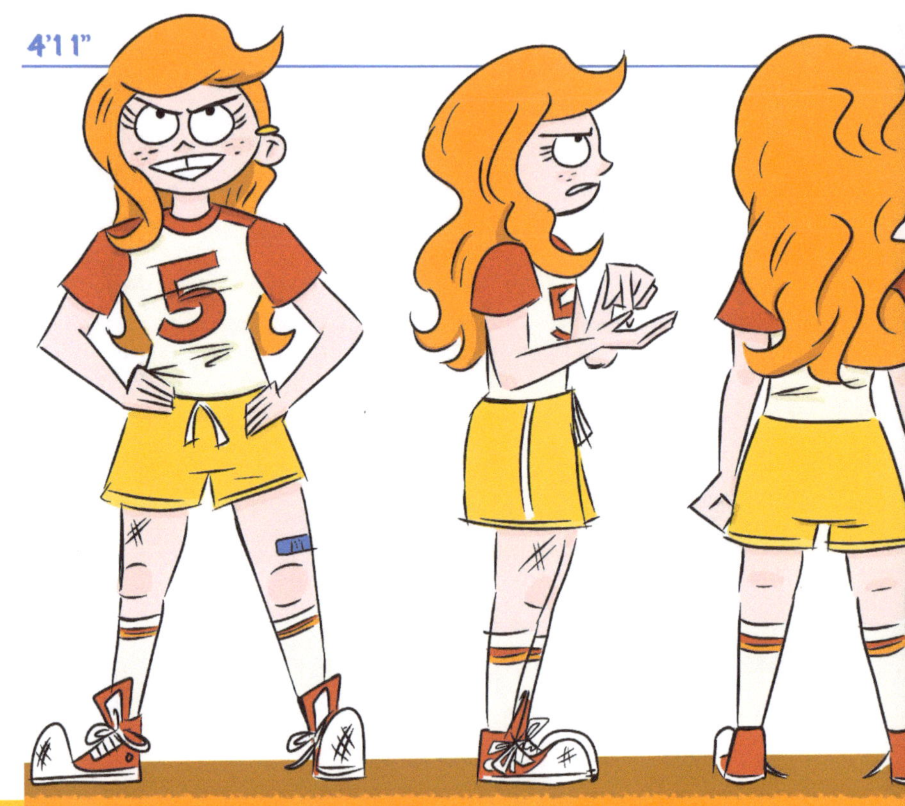

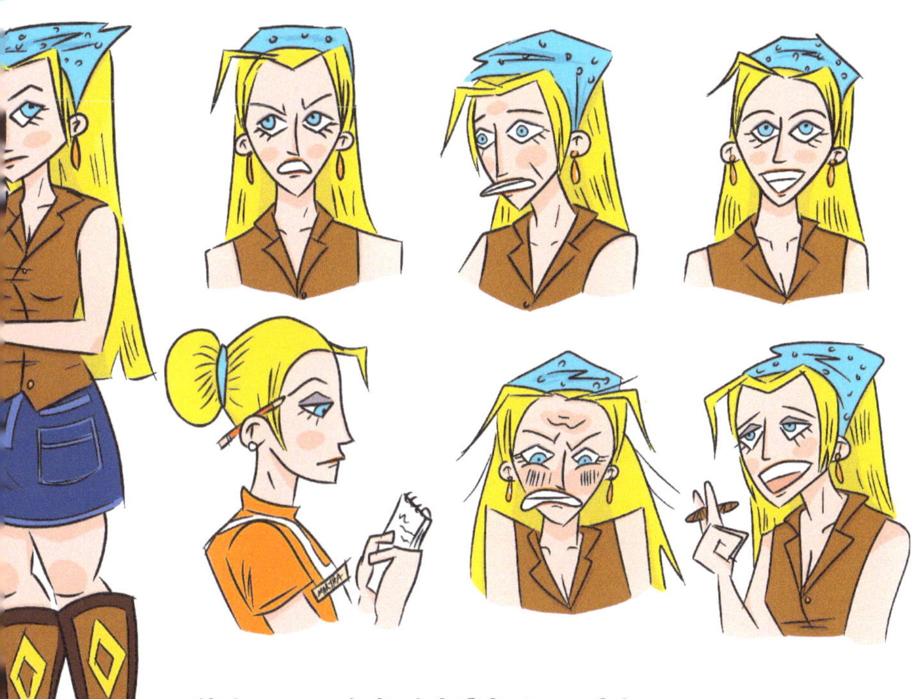

Febuary 14, 1953, Age 21

Martha Reine Dansereau

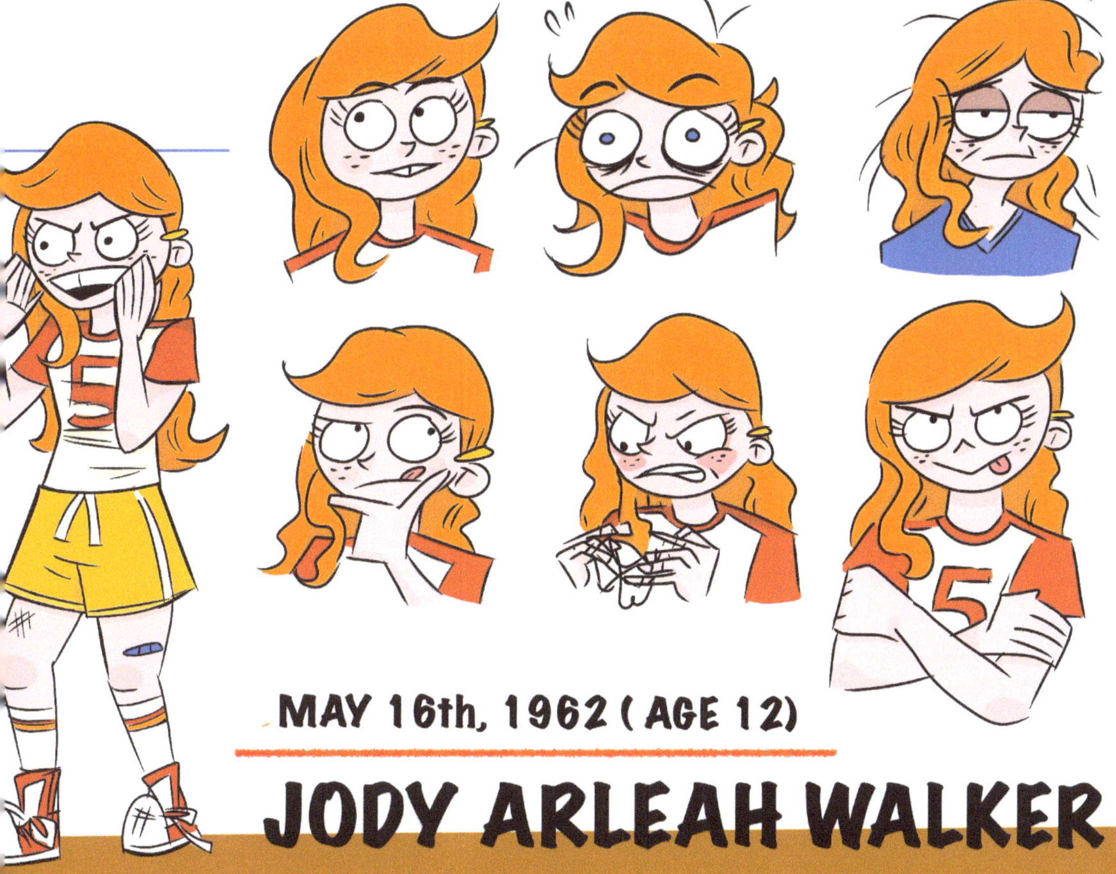

MAY 16th, 1962 (AGE 12)

JODY ARLEAH WALKER

Jody Character Sheet, 4096 x 1714 px, 2023

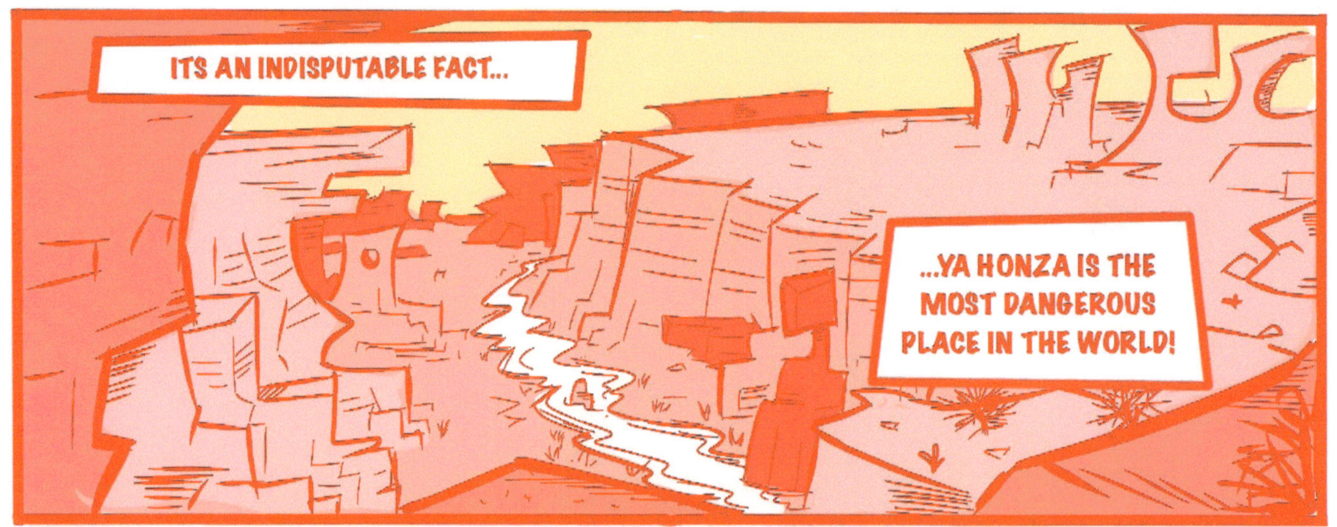

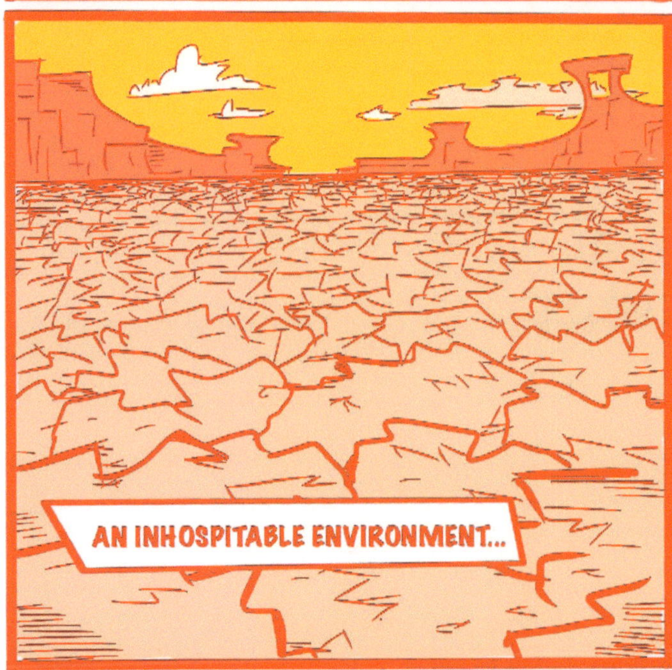

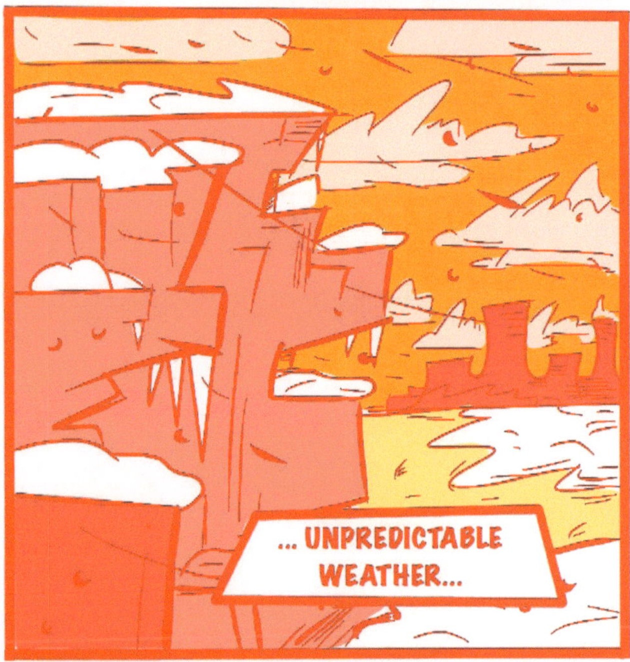

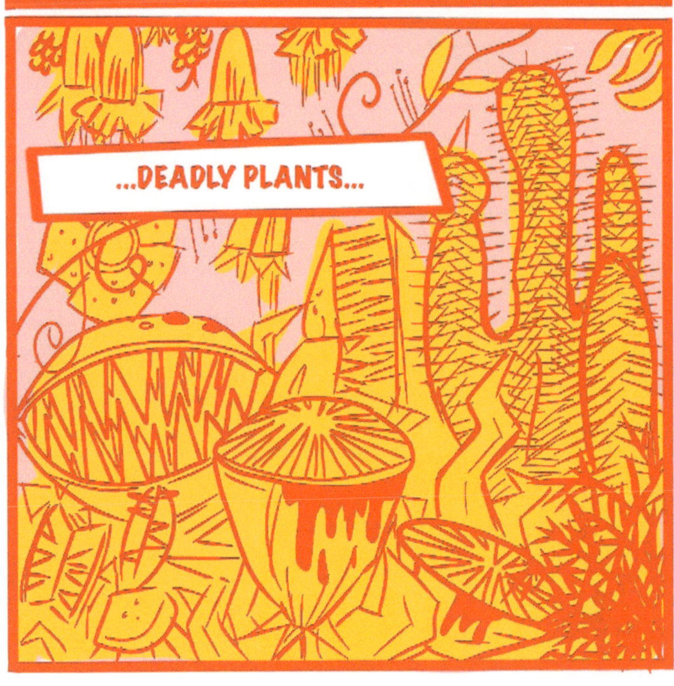

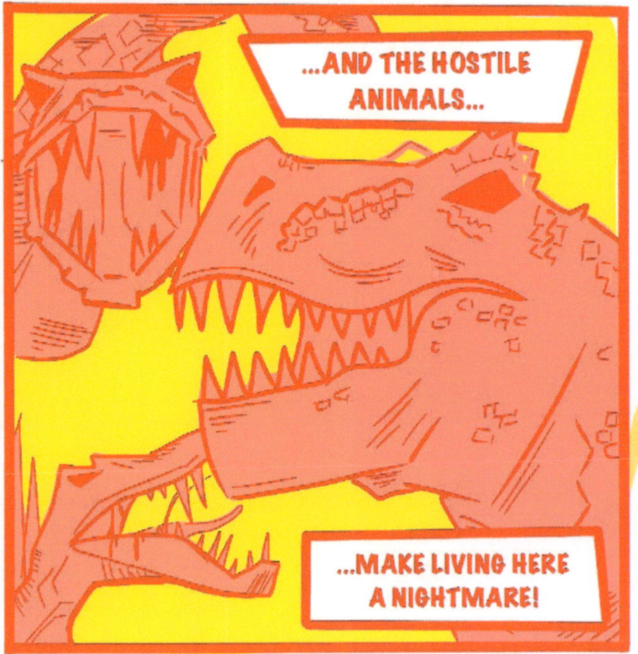

Ya Honza, 8 x 12 in, 2021

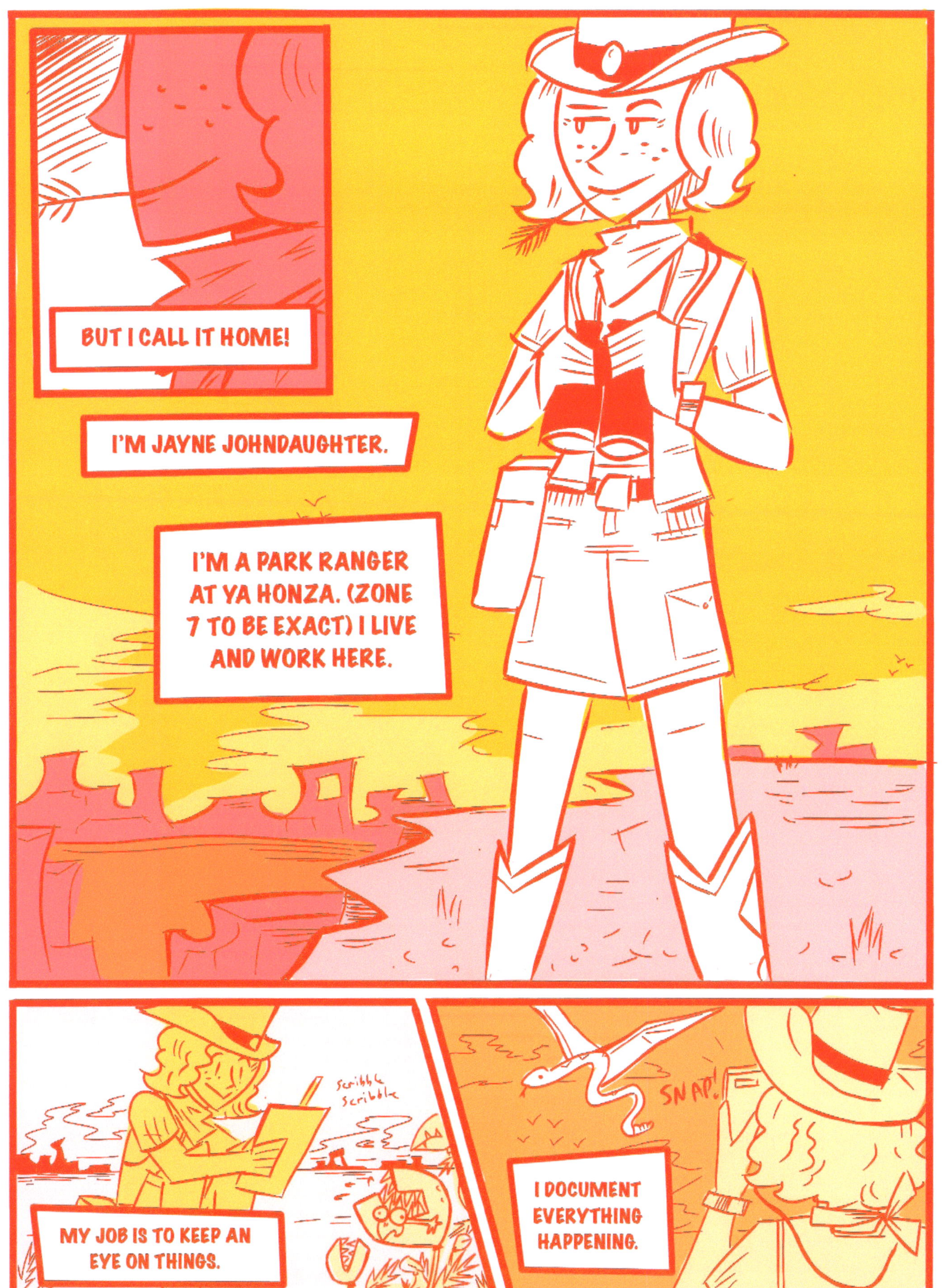

Ya Honza, 8 x 12 in, 2021

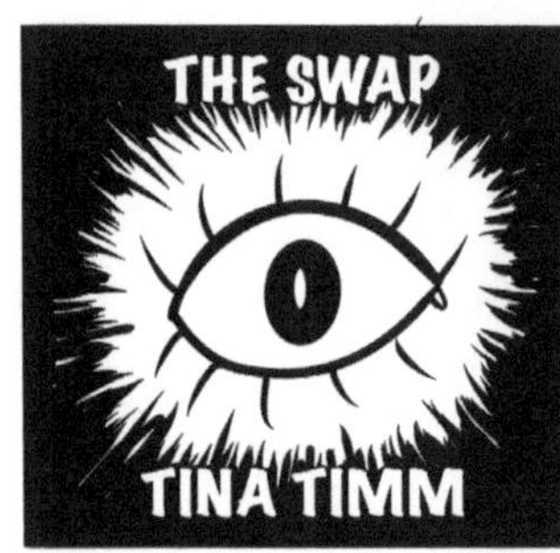

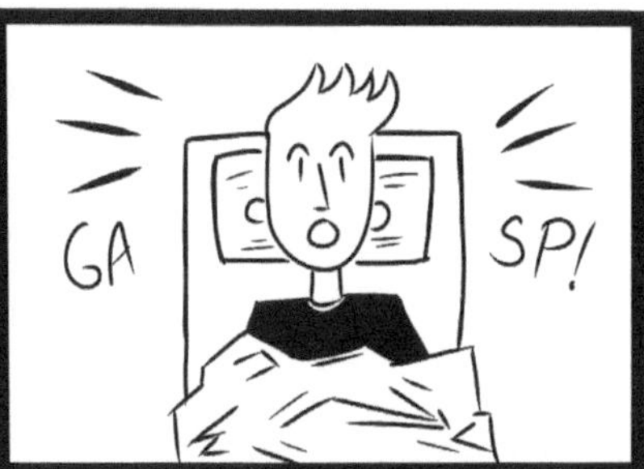

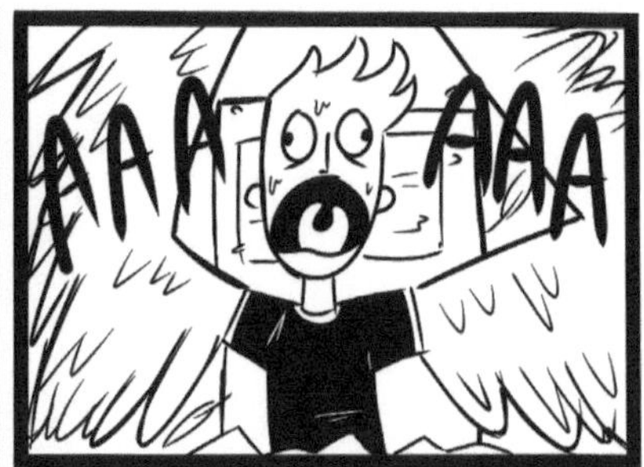

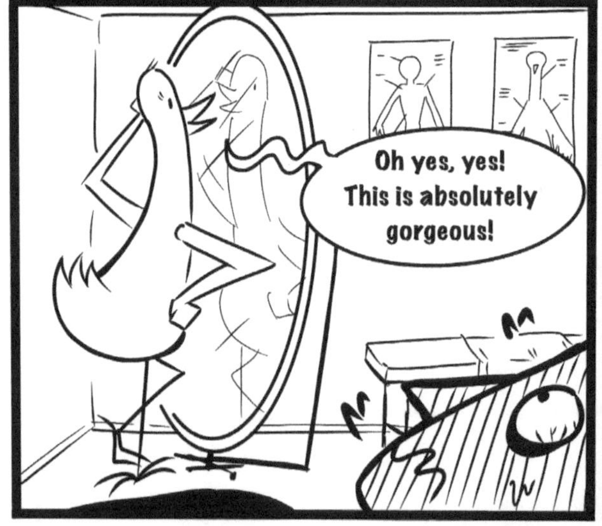

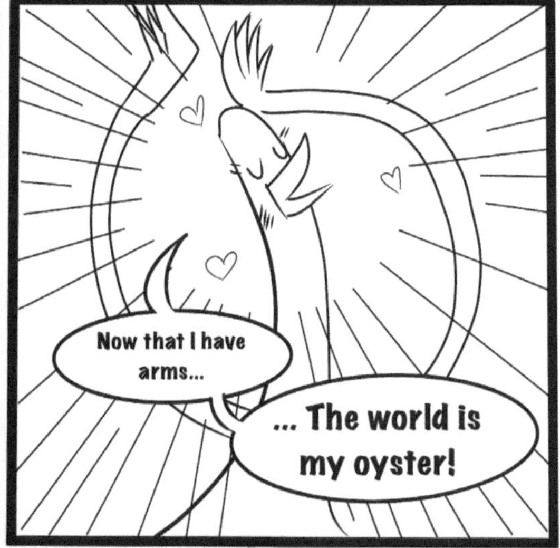

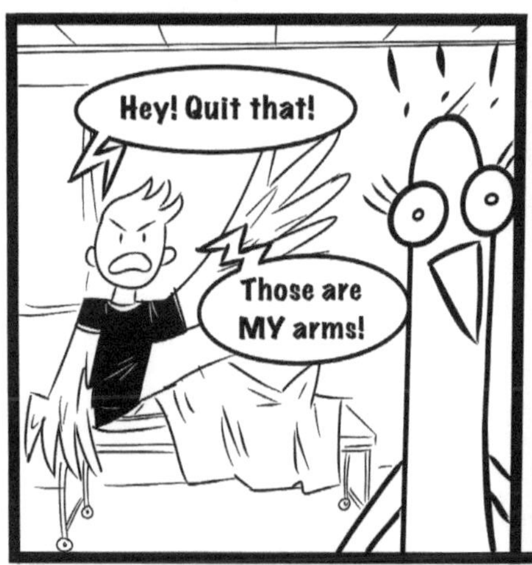

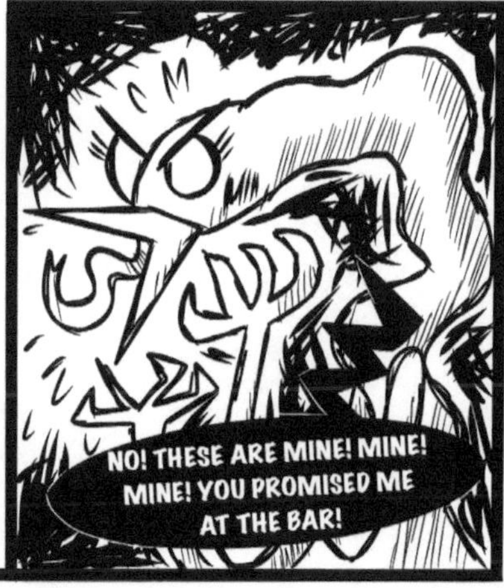

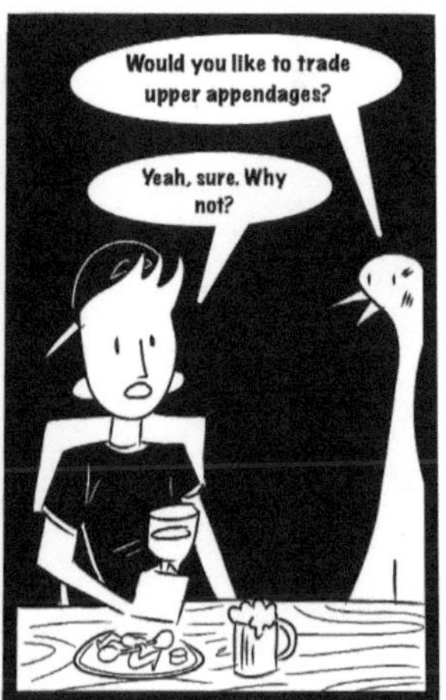

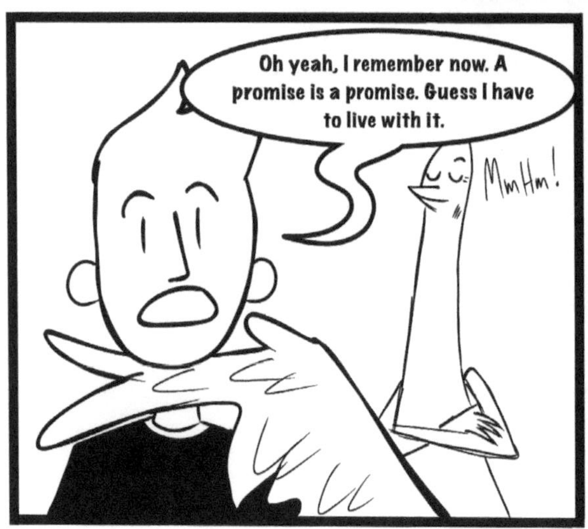

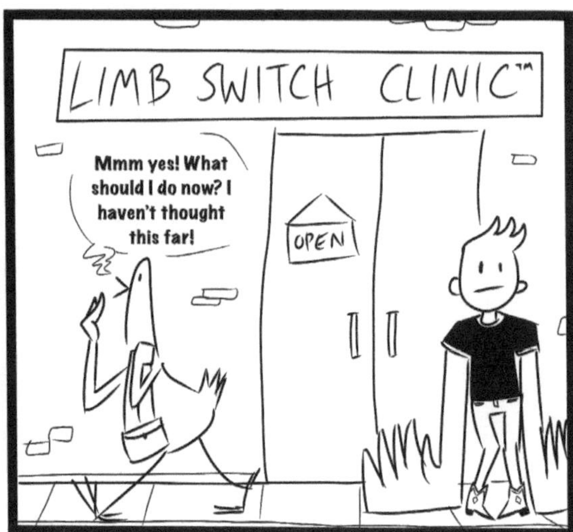

The Swap, 8 x 14 in, 2021

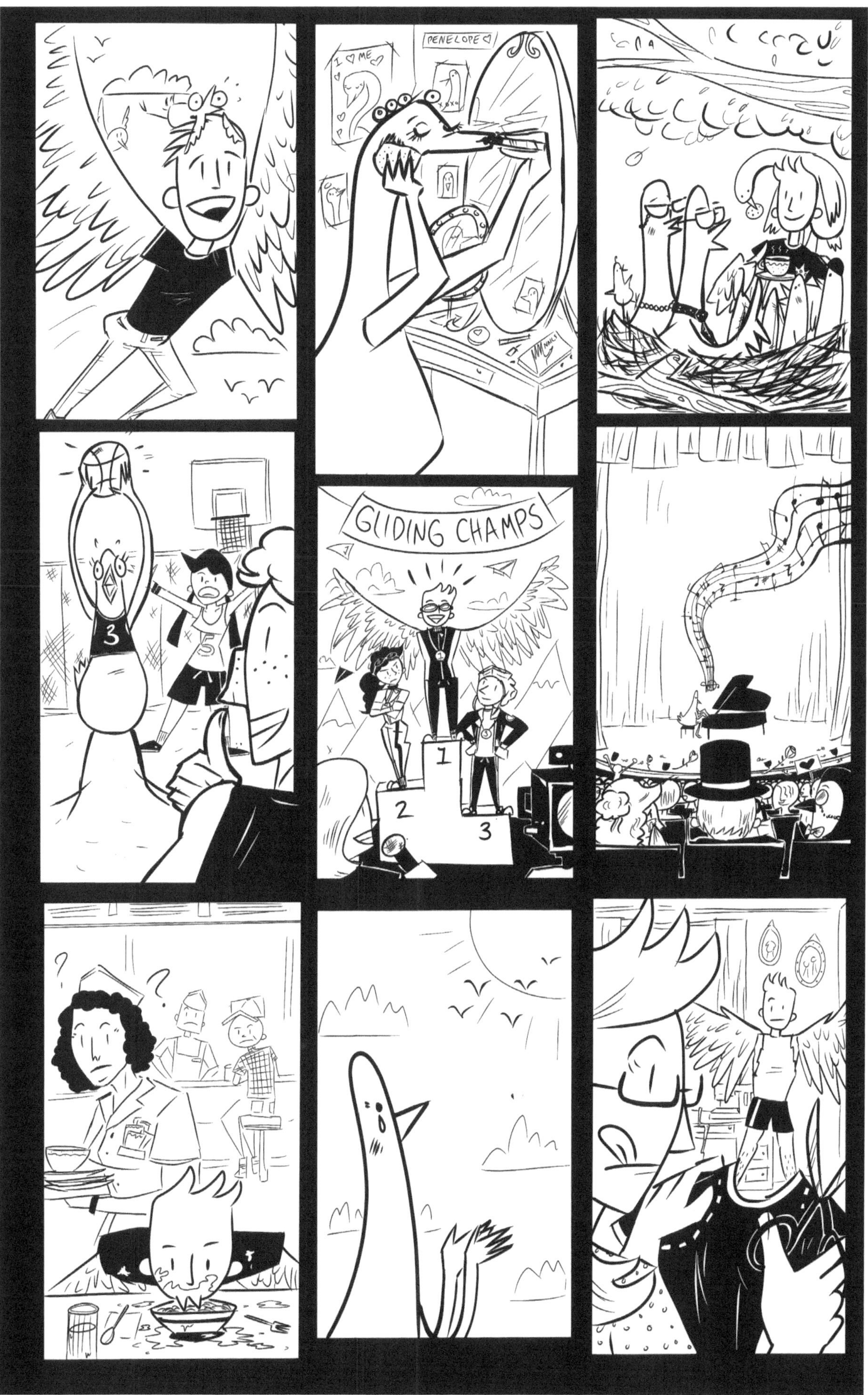

The Swap, 8 x 14 in, 2021

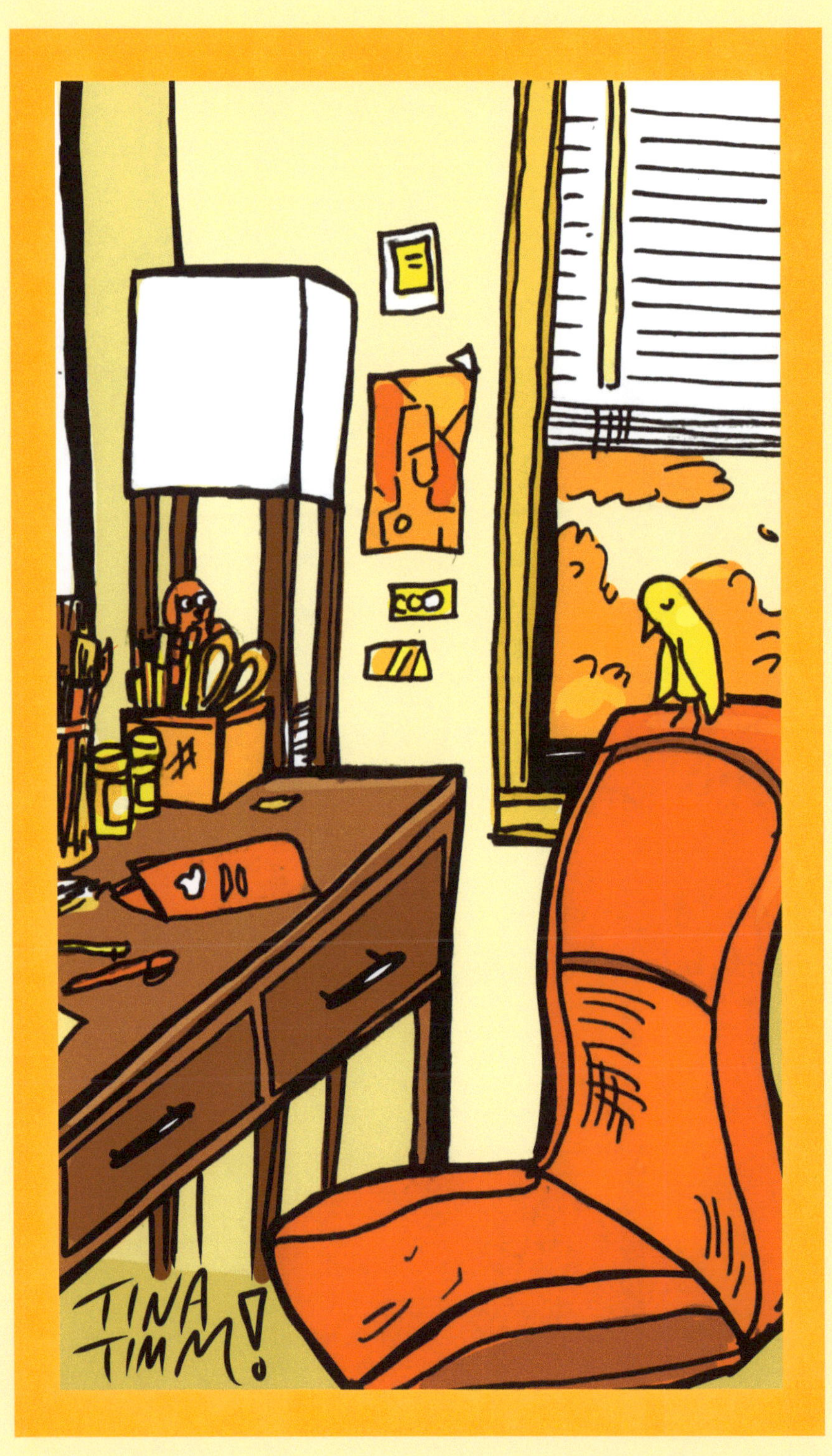
♥ DO
TINA
TIMM!

Tina Timm is a midwestern illustrator and
cartoonist. She graduated from Milwaukee
Institute of Art and Design with an Illustration
major and a communication design minor.

Her digital art is done in Procreate, Adobe Illustrator,
and Adobe Photoshop. Her traditional art is ink,
pencil, marker, watercolor, or acrylic paint. Her
specialty is cartooning and graphic design, but is
always striving to learn new mediums and styles.

On her free time, she loves to go out hiking, cycling, rock
climbing, and urban spelunking. When not outdoors, she
is learning to cook new recipes or is providing for her
parakeet, Peep. She tries to keep herself as busy as
possible and is constantly learning and self-improving.

@flipphoneart3.0   www.flipphoneart/squarespace.com   tinatimm14@gmail.com

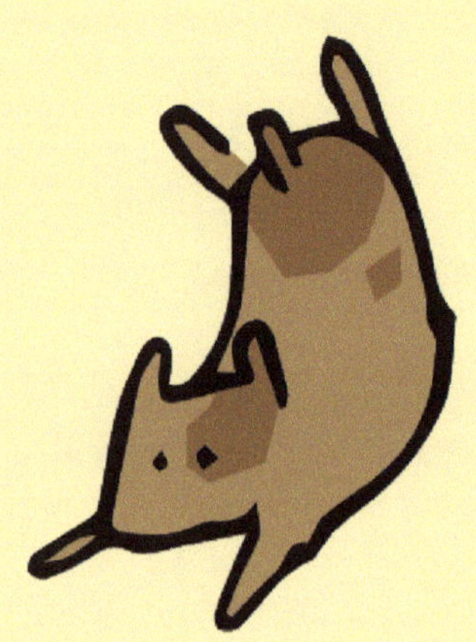